NEW YORK

NEW YORK

HELLO
U.S.A.

by Amy Gelman

Lerner Publications Company

You'll find this picture of a taxicab in New York City at the beginning of each chapter. There are more than 12,000 licensed taxicabs in New York City and about 40,000 licensed taxicab drivers. On an average day, a driver serves 30 passengers and travels 141 miles. Yellow became the official color of licensed taxicabs in 1969.

Cover (left): Horseshoe Falls, Niagara River. Cover (right): The Statue of Liberty, Liberty Island, New York Harbor. Pages 2–3: Manhattan skyline. Page 3: Moonrise over Giant Mountain in the Adirondacks.

Copyright © 2002 by Lerner Publications Company

This book is available in two editions:
Library binding by Lerner Publications Company, a division of Lerner Publishing Group
Soft cover by First Avenue Editions, an imprint of Lerner Publishing Group
241 First Avenue North
Minneapolis, MN 55401 U.S.A.

Website address: www.lernerbooks.com

Library of Congress Cataloging-in-Publication Data

Gelman, Amy, 1961–
    New York / by Amy Gelman. (Rev. and expanded 2nd ed.)
       p.   cm. — (Hello U.S.A.)
    Includes index.
    ISBN: 0–8225–4057–6 (lib. bdg. : alk. paper)
    ISBN: 0–8225–4151–3 (pbk. : alk. paper)
    1. New York (State)—Juvenile literature. [1. New York (State)] I. Title. II. Series.
    F119.3 .G45 2002
    974.7—dc21   2001002446

Manufactured in the United States of America
1 2 3 4 5 6 – JR – 07 06 05 04 03 02

CONTENTS

Chequaqua Falls is one of 19 waterfalls in the heart of New York's Finger Lakes region.

THE LAND

Lakes, Forests, and Mountains

any people think only of New York City when they think of New York. They imagine skyscrapers, bright lights, crowds of people. But the state of New York boasts much more than just its most famous city. Stretching from the Atlantic Ocean to Lake Erie, from the beaches of Long Island to the peaks of the Appalachian Mountains, New York's landscape is varied and lively.

New York borders five northeastern states—Vermont, Massachusetts, Connecticut, New Jersey, and Pennsylvania. Canada lies to the north, and Lake Ontario and Lake Erie, two of the **Great Lakes,** cross New York's northern and western boundaries.

A family enjoys a sunny day at a beach along Lake Ontario at Wescott Beach State Park.

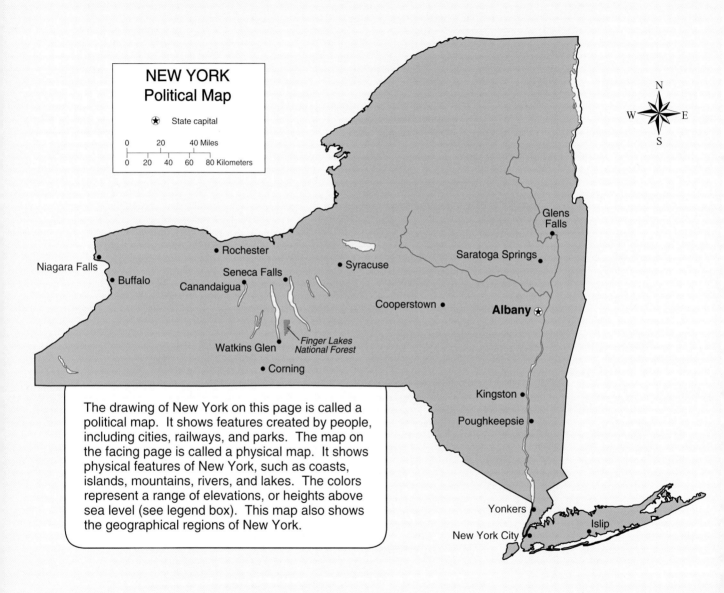

NEW YORK
Political Map

★ State capital

0   20   40 Miles

0   20   40   60   80 Kilometers

Niagara Falls

• Buffalo

• Rochester

Seneca Falls
Canandaigua

• Syracuse

Saratoga Springs

Glens Falls

Cooperstown •

Albany ✪

Watkins Glen

Finger Lakes National Forest

• Corning

Kingston •

Poughkeepsie •

Yonkers

New York City

Islip

N
W   E
S

The drawing of New York on this page is called a political map. It shows features created by people, including cities, railways, and parks. The map on the facing page is called a physical map. It shows physical features of New York, such as coasts, islands, mountains, rivers, and lakes. The colors represent a range of elevations, or heights above sea level (see legend box). This map also shows the geographical regions of New York.

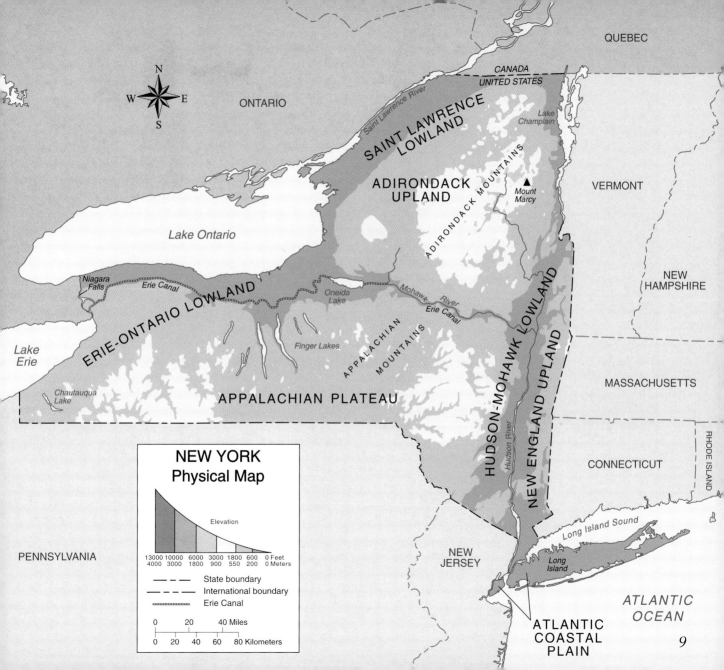

QUEBEC

ONTARIO

Saint Lawrence River

CANADA
UNITED STATES

SAINT LAWRENCE
LOWLAND

Lake Champlain

ADIRONDACK
UPLAND

ADIRONDACK MOUNTAINS

▲ Mount Marcy

VERMONT

Lake Ontario

NEW HAMPSHIRE

Niagara Falls

Erie Canal

ERIE-ONTARIO LOWLAND

Oneida Lake

Mohawk River

Erie Canal

Finger Lakes

Lake Erie

APPALACHIAN MOUNTAINS

HUDSON-MOHAWK LOWLAND

NEW ENGLAND UPLAND

Chautauqua Lake

APPALACHIAN PLATEAU

Hudson River

MASSACHUSETTS

CONNECTICUT

RHODE ISLAND

Long Island Sound

NEW YORK
Physical Map

Elevation

13000 10000 6000 3000 1800 600 0 Feet
4000 3000 1800 900 550 200 0 Meters

— - — State boundary

— - - — International boundary

········ Erie Canal

0   20   40 Miles

0   20   40   60   80 Kilometers

PENNSYLVANIA

NEW JERSEY

Long Island

ATLANTIC
COASTAL
PLAIN

ATLANTIC
OCEAN

9

Glaciers changed the shape of New York's Adirondack Mountains thousands of years ago.

The landscape owes much of its appearance to glaciers, vast blocks of ice that covered the region tens of thousands of years ago. As the glaciers melted, they left their mark on almost everything in their path. They ground their way over ancient mountains such as the Adirondacks, changing their size and shape. The glaciers also carved out hollows in the earth that filled with water to form thousands of lakes around the state.

Over time, glaciers and other natural forces created four types of land in New York—upland, lowland, plateau, and coastal plain.

New York's two upland regions are called the New England Upland and the Adirondack Upland. They are both in the eastern part of the state. Both regions are hilly and thickly forested. New York's highest peak, Mount Marcy (5,344 feet), rises high above the Adirondack Upland.

In New York's lowland regions, farms are a common sight.

Lake Ontario contributes to the fertile soil of the Erie-Ontario Lowland.

New York's lowlands are well suited to farming. The Hudson-Mohawk Lowland is a narrow stretch of rich farmland in the southeastern and east central parts of the state. The rolling Saint Lawrence Lowland and the wide, flat Erie-Ontario Lowland,

Located in the Adirondack Mountains, Ausable Lake is one of New York's thousands of lakes.

both in northern New York, also have fertile soil.

The Appalachian Plateau, a flat, rocky region famous for its snowy winters, covers much of the southern part of the state. The region consists mostly of small towns and has few cities. Its scenery includes the Finger Lakes (a popular vacation area) and many dairy farms.

In southeastern New York lies the Atlantic Coastal Plain. This low, flat region is known for its beautiful ocean beaches. It includes three of New York City's five **boroughs** (counties)—Queens, Brooklyn, and Staten Island.

Of New York's many rivers, the best known are probably the Hudson and the Mohawk, in the eastern part of the state, and the Saint Lawrence, on the border between New York and Canada. Long before people had cars or trains, they used these rivers for trade and travel.

New Yorkers enjoy several thousand lakes. The largest lake that is entirely within the state's borders is Lake Oneida, near Syracuse.

Like most places in New York, the Hudson River Valley experiences snowy winters.

New York receives a moderate amount of rainfall year round.

Some parts of New York have a mild climate and moderate amounts of precipitation (rain, snow, sleet, and hail) all year round. But people in northern New York endure long winters with below-freezing temperatures. Huge amounts of snow—often more than 100 inches in a season—fall on western New York in winter.

In the New York City area, summers are often hot and humid, with temperatures climbing to 95° F or higher. Farther inland, summers are cooler, and by August, evenings can become chilly.

The varying landscapes in New York are home to lots of different animals. Beavers, opossums, and chipmunks scurry around the state's countryside. Larger animals such as red foxes and white-tailed deer live there too.

Crabs, lobsters, whales, sharks, and bluefish are some of the creatures that swim in New York's coastal waters. Many birds, including egrets and terns, wade in the marshes near the state's seashore.

Red fox cubs make their home in New York's countryside.

Black-eyed Susans and other flowers grow wild in New York.

New York's state flower, the rose, grows wild in some areas, and so do black-eyed Susans and Indian pipes, among many other plants. More than 50 percent of New York is covered with forest, and about 150 types of trees—including sugar maples, beeches, oaks, balsam firs, pines, and spruces— grow there.

Building the Empire State

People probably first settled in the area that became New York about 10,000 years ago, after the glaciers that once covered the area had melted. Scientists have found pieces of tools and weapons that these people used and mounds of earth where they buried their dead. But no one knows very much about them. Their descendants are the people called Native Americans, or Indians.

By the time the first people from Europe came to the area, in the 1500s, two main groups of Indians lived there. The people of one of the groups spoke Algonquian languages, and most of them farmed and hunted near the Hudson and Saint Lawrence Rivers. These people included the Mahican, the Montauk, the Wappinger, and the Delaware.

The other group, the Iroquois, lived farther west. The Iroquois also farmed, growing crops such as corn and tobacco. Warfare was important to the Iroquois and served as a way for young men to prove they were strong and powerful.

During the 1400s, five Iroquois nations formed a group known as the Iroquois Confederacy. The members of the Confederacy were the Mohawk, the Seneca, the Oneida, the Cayuga, and the Onondaga. They agreed to keep peace among themselves and to protect each other from enemies.

About 1524 Giovanni da Verrazano, an Italian explorer, sailed into the harbor of what later became New York City. Verrazano returned to Europe, but other Europeans followed in the next century. Some of them stayed and changed the lives of New York's Indians forever.

Tools like these were probably used by the first people who lived in the New York area.

In 1609 Samuel de Champlain, a French explorer, set up a fur-trading post in Quebec, Canada, not far from what later became northern New York. There, he traded with Algonquian tribes from the region. Champlain exchanged European goods for the pelts of beavers, minks, and other furry animals that thrived throughout the area.

In turn, the Algonquian tribes traded some of the French goods with the Iroquois Confederacy, especially with the Mohawk. The Iroquois also took goods by force from the Algonquian tribes who traded with Champlain.

During the 1700s, Mohawk Indians made birchbark canoes to navigate the area's many waterways.

An early European settler created this drawing of an Iroquois warrior.

Also in 1609, an Englishman named Henry Hudson, working for the Dutch government, sailed up the long river that was later named for him. Like many explorers at the time, he was looking for a new way to get from Europe to Asia. Hudson quickly realized that he had not found a passageway to Asia. He liked the territory, though, and found that the Mahican who lived there were willing to trade with Europeans.

The mighty Hudson River is named after Henry Hudson, who explored the river and the area around it in 1609.

In 1625 the Dutch established a settlement at the mouth of the Hudson River. They called it New Amsterdam.

't Fort nieuw Amsterdam op de Manhatans

Hudson claimed the area for the Dutch, who called it New Netherland. Soon, some Dutch businessmen decided to send Dutch citizens to establish a settlement, or **colony,** in the region. By settling on the land, the Dutch would strengthen their claim of ownership. Thirty Dutch families established a colony at Fort Orange (later Albany) in 1624.

The Dutch colonists were joined by people from the British-run colonies of Connecticut and Massachusetts Bay. Those colonies did not let everyone practice religion freely, so many people left. People from all over Europe also settled in New Netherland.

Peter Stuyvesant was New Netherland's governor from 1647 to 1664.

In addition, the Dutch brought black people from Africa to the colony to be slaves. So although the Dutch government controlled the colony, not all of its people were Dutch. People of many different religions, nationalities, and races lived there.

In 1663 King Charles II of Britain decided to take over the colony of New Netherland. He wanted to control New Amsterdam (later New York City), which was an important trading port. In 1664 he sent four British warships into New Amsterdam harbor and gave his brother James a charter claiming the territory.

Peter Stuyvesant, New Netherland's governor, realized the colonists could not defeat the British forces. The Dutch peacefully gave up their claim to New Netherland, and British settlers promptly renamed it New York, after James, Duke of York.

During the French and Indian Wars, Joseph Brant, or Thayendanegea, led fellow Iroquois warriors in battles against the British.

Both the French and the British wanted to profit from the furs they bought from the Indians. From 1689 to 1763, Britain and France fought a series of wars, often called the French and Indian Wars. Each country hoped to gain complete control of the territory and its fur trade. Because many important trading posts were located in what later became New York, several battles in the French and Indian Wars were fought there.

Most Indians fought on one side or the other in the wars, usually siding with their European trading partners. Many of the Indians who lived in New York fought each other as well. By this time, the five original Iroquois nations had added the Tuscarora, originally from North Carolina, to the league.

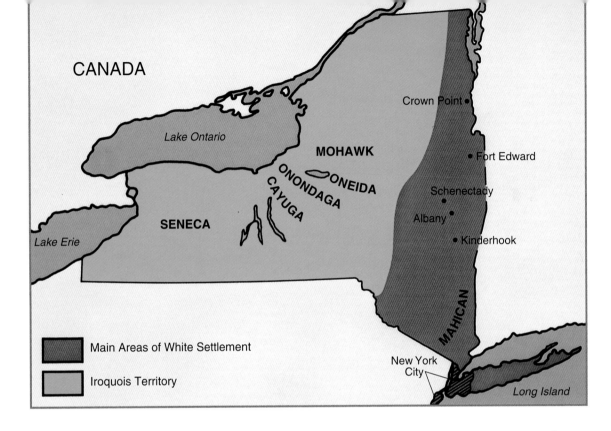

CANADA

Lake Ontario

Crown Point •

MOHAWK

ONEIDA

ONONDAGA

CAYUGA

SENECA

• Fort Edward

Schenectady
•

Albany •

• Kinderhook

Lake Erie

MAHICAN

New York
City

Long Island

Main Areas of White Settlement

Iroquois Territory

This map shows some of the main cities in the colony of New York and the major tribes in the region. In the mid-1700s, most Europeans still lived in the eastern part of New York. The Iroquois controlled the western part.

The French and Indian Wars ended in 1763. The long, trying wars had cost a great deal of money, and the British looked for ways to help pay for the war. One way was to make the American colonists pay more taxes to the British government. These new taxes would not only bring money into Britain, they would also remind the colonists that the British still controlled the colonies.

The taxes made many New Yorkers angry. Why should the people of New York, many of whom were not even British, have to pay the cost of Britain's wars? In 1765 people from 9 of the 13 British colonies agreed not to buy any British goods—to **boycott** them—until the government canceled the taxes.

The British did take back most of the new taxes, and some New Yorkers were satisfied that the boycott of British goods had succeeded. Some of these New Yorkers were **Loyalists,** people who supported the British government. But other New Yorkers, and many people throughout the colonies, wanted to end British control forever. They decided to fight for independence.

In 1775 colonial forces, calling themselves the Continental Army, entered the American War of Independence against the British. The following year, representatives from all 13 British colonies signed the Declaration of Independence. It stated that the colonies were free from British rule. But the Declaration of Independence didn't end the war.

The British army captured Long Island and New York City in 1776. They occupied the area throughout the war. But the colonists fought hard. Even with the help of Iroquois, Montauk, and other Indian soldiers, the British could not take over all of New York. The first major colonial victory occurred at the Battle of Saratoga, in northeastern New York, in 1777.

The defeat of the colonists in the Battle of Long Island allowed the British to take over New York City.

During the Revolutionary War, Fort Ticonderoga was an important military base.

With help from the French, and the many Indians who supported the French, the colonists eventually won the war. The British surrendered in 1781, and the colonists formed a new country—the United States of America. The two sides had fought many battles on New York soil, and many New Yorkers—colonists and Indians—had died in the fighting.

During the war, American troops had destroyed many Iroquois villages, and some Iroquois who had fought with the British fled to Canada.

The War of 1812

Only 31 years after the War of Independence ended, New York was again a battleground in a fight against the British—the War of 1812. After the War of Independence, many British sailors left the British navy and went to work on U.S. ships. The British began stopping ships at sea and forcing any British-born sailors on board to return to the British navy.

To get the British to stop stealing sailors from U.S. ships, the United States refused to buy anything from Britain. When the British continued to steal sailors, the U.S. Congress declared war on Britain.

Many British troops were stationed in Canada, so towns near New York's Canadian border became major military bases for U.S. troops. New York contributed large numbers of ships and troops to the U.S. cause. The fighting ended in 1814 with the signing of the Treaty of Ghent.

After the war, the U.S. government forced the Iroquois who remained in New York to sell their land and move to **reservations,** small parcels of land reserved for Indians.

Control of New York now belonged to the former colonists. In 1788 they joined the new nation as its 11th state. They then turned to developing their state. The government gradually sold the land that it had taken from the Iroquois. People who had fought in the war were among the first white people to buy this newly available land. They established towns and farmed the fertile soil.

In the early 1800s, Governor DeWitt Clinton persuaded the state government to build a canal to connect Lake Erie with the Hudson River. The Erie Canal, completed in 1825, made it easy to ship goods such as lumber, leather, and flour from the Midwest and western New York to the port at New York City. From there the products were sent overseas to be sold. Banks were opened in New York City to manage the money that buyers and sellers made.

After its opening in 1825, the Erie Canal helped make New York an important center of manufacturing and business.

With land and jobs available all over the state, New York's population grew and grew, especially in the cities. People came from other parts of the United States. **Immigrants**—people from other countries—moved to New York. Soon New York had more citizens than any state in the country.

The large population provided many workers for New York's factories, which produced a wide variety of goods, including flour, lumber, textiles (cloth), and leather goods. As farms and factories churned out more products and made more money, and as more banks and financial companies were opened to manage that money, New York became the country's center of trade, finance, and manufacturing.

Although slavery had been abolished in New York since 1827, not all New Yorkers were opposed to it. In July 1863, people protested against fighting for the North in the Civil War. They rioted in New York City's streets and burned buildings, including the homes of many black people.

In the 1860s, during the Civil War, New York joined the Northern side, which fought to end slavery. Black people in New York didn't have the same rights as white people, but slavery had been outlawed in New York since 1827. Many New Yorkers were against slavery, and the state helped the North defeat the South by sending more men to fight than any other state.

The Statue of Liberty was built in France between 1875 and 1884. It has greeted immigrants for over a century with the hope of a better life in the United States of America.

As New York's population continued to grow throughout the 1800s, it became more and more varied. Immigrants were arriving in greater numbers and from more places than ever before. Some people called New York a **melting pot,** because it contained so many different "ingredients," or types of people.

In the early 1900s, immigrants to New York City formed many ethnic neighborhoods such as this one, known as Little Italy.

First from Ireland, then from Italy, Poland, Germany, and elsewhere in Europe, hundreds of thousands of immigrants poured into the state. Even most immigrants who settled in other parts of the United States came through New York first. Government officials checked in new arrivals to the country at Ellis Island, an immigration station in New York Harbor.

In 1990 the Ellis Island immigration station in New York City was made into a museum.

At the turn of the century many people in New York worked in factories such as General Electric's Schenectady Works.

By 1900 one out of every three New Yorkers had been born in a foreign country. The newcomers often found jobs in the state's many factories, making different types of goods ranging from sewing machines to magazines, from cameras to clothes.

Hunger and worries about the future plagued many people who could not find work during the Great Depression.

New York City's stock exchange was the center of the country's financial activity. There, people bought and sold **stocks,** or shares in the ownership of businesses. But in 1929, the prices of shares on the stock exchange crashed, or fell drastically. The stocks became nearly worthless, and stockholders lost huge amounts of money.

President Franklin D. Roosevelt waves from a train as it arrives in Hyde Park, New York.

The stock market crash led to a period in the 1930s known as the Great Depression. When stock owners lost so much money, many businesses shut down. Stores closed down because people didn't want to spend the little money they had. Thousands of New Yorkers, like others across the land, lost jobs and had little money for food, clothing, and other needs.

Franklin D. Roosevelt, New York's governor, believed that the government should help its needy citizens. He created programs to provide food and medical care for poor families and to create jobs for people who were out of work.

In 1932 Roosevelt was elected president—the fifth U.S. president from New York. As president, he developed more programs, known as the New Deal, to help people who were suffering because of the Great Depression. Through the New Deal, Roosevelt helped lead his home state, and the country, out of the Great Depression. World War II (1939–45) further boosted the economy in the early 1940s. New York's factories bustled to prepare equipment for the troops overseas.

By the late 1940s, New York had returned to its position as the country's leader in finance and manufacturing. In the following decades, some industries began leaving New York for states with cheaper property and lower taxes, taking thousands of jobs with them. But most companies stayed, and New York is still one of the world's major business, finance, and manufacturing centers.

In recent years, New Yorkers have seen a decrease in crime. But poverty and homelessness remain widespread in New York's cities, and the state's many races and ethnic groups do not always get along with each other. Despite these challenges, most New Yorkers find their state an exciting place to live, work, and play.

In 2000 New York made history by becoming the first state to elect a First Lady to public office. New Yorkers elected Hillary Rodham Clinton to represent them in the U.S. Senate.

New York has had many different capitals over the years, including the cities of Kingston, Poughkeepsie, and New York City. Albany didn't become the state capital until 1797. The capitol building *(below)* was built in 1879.

PEOPLE & ECONOMY

America's Melting Pot

or almost as long as people have lived there, New York has had a varied population. Long before the Duke of York gave the area his name, numerous Native American tribes, each speaking a different language and following a different way of life, made their homes there. The millions of people—almost 19 million—who live in New York have their origins in countries all over the world.

Immigrants are still coming to New York in large numbers. More than 15 percent of New Yorkers were born in foreign countries. Many of the newest immigrants come from Latin America and Asia, but the largest number of New Yorkers born outside the United States come from the Dominican Republic,

Students in New York work on a group project.

Italy, Jamaica, Russia, Germany, Poland, and Haiti.
  New York also has about 3 million African
American residents, more than any other state in
the country. More Jewish people live in New York
than in any other state. Hispanics make up about
15 percent of the state's population. More than
80,000 Native Americans call New York home.

Albany is the sixth largest city in New York. It is also the capital.

Most New Yorkers live in cities. New York City is the largest city in the country, with over 8 million people, and almost half of all New Yorkers live in the New York City area. Most other residents live in or near the state's other large cities, which include Buffalo, Rochester, and Syracuse. Only about 15 percent of New Yorkers live in small villages or other **rural** areas.

People often come to New York from other states and countries to join family members who are already living there. But they also come because

New York continues to be the business and cultural capital of the country and one of the most exciting places to live in the world.

The people who have moved to New York over the years have brought elements of their backgrounds to the state, creating a unique mix of cultures. As a result, New York can claim many of the greatest, and most varied, artistic opportunities in the country.

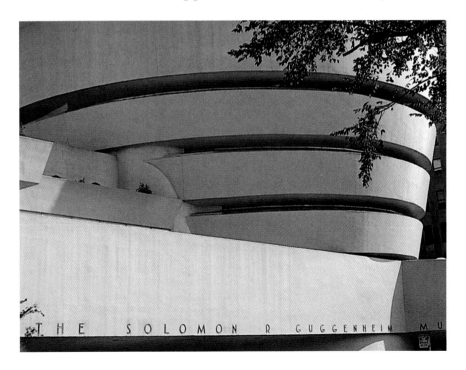

New York City's Guggenheim Museum is famous for its unusual shape and its fine collection of modern art.

A glass dome stands outside the Adirondack Museum in Blue Mountain Lake, New York. New York has many museums and cultural events for residents and visitors to enjoy.

New York City's theaters are so famous that Broadway, the street that houses many of the theaters, has come to mean "theater." The city boasts dozens of museums and galleries, including the Metropolitan Museum of Art, the country's largest art museum.

People who enjoy dance can watch a wide variety in New York City, from the traditional American Ballet Theatre to the modern Alvin Ailey Dance Company. For music lovers, there are concert halls such as the Metropolitan Opera House and night-clubs offering nearly every type of music imaginable.

Elsewhere in the state, more cultural opportunities are available. Several cities, including Buffalo and Albany, have their own orchestras. Museums around the state include the International Museum of Photography in Rochester, the Corning Glass Center in Corning, and the National Baseball Hall of Fame in Cooperstown.

New Yorkers who like sports are lucky. Their state has two professional baseball teams, the New York Yankees and the New York Mets.

The New York Yankees are a favorite team in New York. They have an excellent record, including several World Series wins.

Many fans in New York enjoy watching the Buffalo Bills football team.

Sports fans can also follow football's Buffalo Bills, New York Jets, and New York Giants. Three hockey teams, the New York Rangers, the New York Islanders, and the Buffalo Sabres, play in the state. Basketball fans can root for the New York Knicks or the New York Liberty.

When they're not watching one of the state's sports teams, some New Yorkers enjoy fishing, boating, and swimming at the state's ocean beaches or at its lakes. Many New Yorkers hike in the summer or ski in the winter.

Many of the nation's major financial companies are found in the Wall Street area, at the southern tip of Manhattan Island.

On any weekday morning in any of New York's cities, thousands of people crowd the streets as they rush off to work. What do all those people, and the millions of other working New Yorkers, do for a living? About 71 percent of them work in jobs that provide services to people.

The best-known service industry in New York is finance and banking. New York City is home to the New York Stock Exchange and to many other financial companies. Many New Yorkers work in other service jobs such as advertising, real estate (the buying and selling of property), and insurance (which protects people and their possessions). The government is the second largest employer in New York, claiming 14 percent of workers.

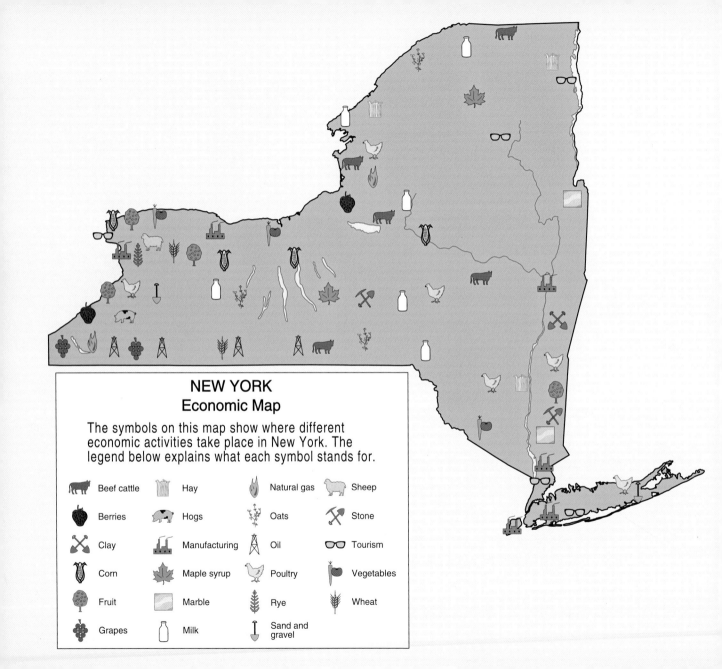

NEW YORK
Economic Map

The symbols on this map show where different economic activities take place in New York. The legend below explains what each symbol stands for.

	Beef cattle		Hay		Natural gas		Sheep
	Berries		Hogs		Oats		Stone
	Clay		Manufacturing		Oil		Tourism
	Corn		Maple syrup		Poultry		Vegetables
	Fruit		Marble		Rye		Wheat
	Grapes		Milk		Sand and gravel		

Grain is held in huge containers called elevators near a shipping port in Buffalo.

Workers in New York's cities make a wide variety of goods, from books to clothing, cameras to computers. In fact, manufacturing provides about 11 percent of the money made in New York every year. New York is the country's second biggest producer of manufactured goods. Only California makes more goods each year.

Some of the state's main manufacturing cities include Rochester, famous for photographic equipment, and Buffalo, where mill workers grind more flour than in any other city in the world. In Syracuse, electrical equipment and automobile parts are made. New York City's workers make more books, magazines, and other printed materials than workers in any other city in the nation.

A worker in an apple orchard gathers one of New York's most important agricultural products.

Farming is important to New York's economy, although not as important as it was in the mid-1800s, when wheat from New York was sold all over the country and in Europe. Milk is the state's leading agricultural product, but beef cattle, hay, corn, and fruit are widely produced too. New York is among the nation's leaders in producing apples—the state's biggest crop—and grapes.

Mining is not a major industry in New York. But New York's land yields many different mineral products, including limestone, salt, sand, and gravel. New York is a leader in natural gas, garnet, lead, and silver.

Tourism is vital to New York's economy. New York City's sights, such as the Statue of Liberty and the Empire State Building, are famous worldwide. Many newlyweds spend their honeymoons at Niagara Falls in western New York. Other tourists admire the scenery of the Finger Lakes or the Adirondack Mountains. With its beauty, excitement, and variety, New York has something for all to enjoy.

Every year countless tourists are attracted to the spectacular Niagara Falls.

Going to Waste?

hether they like exciting cities or beautiful countryside, people find many reasons to live in New York, and that's why so many people live there. But every day, all those people produce garbage—at work, at school, at home, and elsewhere.

In fact, each New Yorker makes more than 5 pounds of garbage, or solid waste, a day. With almost 19 million people in the state, that amounts to a lot of garbage. Since most of the state's land is used by people, New Yorkers have a hard time finding enough places to put all that waste.

New Yorkers send most of their solid waste to **landfills,** areas of land where garbage is buried, and they've done so for many years. Recently, though, some of New York's landfills have begun to run out of room. Others have been closed because they polluted the state's **groundwater,** the water supply below the earth's surface.

Landfills pollute groundwater when rotting garbage mixes with rainwater to create a liquid called **leachate.** Leachate is full of materials that pollute. The state government could choose to build new landfills, safe ones that won't leak. But that would be expensive, and New York has very little room to build new landfills.

New Yorkers could also ship their garbage to landfills in other states. But shipping garbage is expensive, especially since landfills in states close to New York are overcrowded too, and waste would have to be sent a long distance.

Garbage is a big problem in New York. Citizens must be aware of ways to cut back on solid waste.

And few states are willing to take New York's garbage. Many New Yorkers discovered this in 1987, when the garbage barge *Mobro*, crammed with more than 3,000 tons of solid waste, left New York Harbor in search of a place to deposit its cargo.

The garbage came from the town of Islip, New York, but Islip's landfill was already full. After sailing for two months without finding any state willing to take the garbage, the barge returned to New York.

Freshkills on Staten Island is one of many overcrowded landfills in New York. Because many landfills are closing, the state is looking for other ways to dispose of its garbage.

The *Mobro's* garbage was burned eventually. Burning is not usually a good way to dispose of waste, however, because the smoke pollutes the air. In addition, plastics and other materials can produce dangerous chemicals when they are burned. But if landfills are full and people don't want to burn waste, what can New Yorkers do with their garbage?

One way to deal with some of it is to recycle. Recycling is collecting and processing garbage for reuse. New York law requires people to separate recyclable garbage, such as newspapers and glass, from non-recyclable items. New Yorkers have to pay a deposit when they buy drinks in cans and bottles. They get their money back if they return the empty can or bottle to the store for recycling.

Workers unload garbage at a New York landfill.

New Yorkers are required to recycle garbage that can be made into new products.

Recycling is better than burning garbage or storing it in landfills, but many New Yorkers feel that it's important to concentrate on finding ways to produce less garbage in the first place.

New Yorkers can find many ways to do this. They can avoid buying disposable products—items that are thrown away after they're used once. Simply reusing things—writing on both sides of a sheet of paper, sharing a magazine with friends instead of each person buying a copy, or cleaning out an empty jar to use for storage—can also cut down the amount of garbage produced.

Barges carry some of New York's garbage to landfills in other states.

New York's solid waste problem is not going to disappear, but it is getting better. About 39 percent of New York's garbage is recycled, and that amount continues to increase. If everyone in New York tries to make less garbage, the state will be a cleaner, safer, and more pleasant place for the millions of people who live there.

Special Note

On September 11, 2001, New York City's World Trade Center was destroyed. Passenger planes that had been hijacked by terrorists crashed into the center's two towers. Soon after, both towers collapsed. Thousands of people died in the disaster.

The same day, another hijacked plane crashed into the Pentagon, the U.S. defense headquarters, near Washington, D.C. A fourth hijacked plane crashed in rural Pennsylvania. These attacks were the worst terrorist actions in history. They caused greater damage and loss of life than the Japanese attack on Pearl Harbor in the Hawaiian Islands in 1941.

New Yorkers and other Americans came together to respond to the disaster at the World Trade Center. Rescue workers rushed to the scene, and many lost their lives. In the days that followed, Mayor Rudolph Giuliani led the city's recovery efforts. The nation united to face the tragedy and an uncertain future.

©Reuters NewMedia Inc./CORBIS

Rescue workers near the wreckage of the World Trade Center. The destruction of the towers changed the Manhattan skyline (pictured on pages 2-3) forever.

ALL ABOUT NEW YORK

Fun Facts

New York City has the longest subway system in the country. If all the subway tracks in New York City were laid end to end, they would stretch all the way to Chicago, Illinois—a distance of 656 miles.

The Dutch people who settled in New York in the 1600s left their mark on the English language. Some familiar English words that come from Dutch include *cookie, yacht,* and *boss.*

New York City was the first capital of the United States. The nation's first congress held its meetings in New York City from 1785 to 1790.

Hot dogs were first sold under the name "dachshund sausages," on Coney Island in Brooklyn, New York, in 1871. In 1901 cartoonist Thomas A. Dorgan drew a cartoon of barking dachshund sausages. Since he didn't know how to spell "dachshund," Dorgan called them "hot dogs," and the name stuck.

Amelia Bloomer lived in Seneca Falls, New York, in the mid-1800s. At that time, American women didn't have the same rights as men. But Bloomer believed that women should be allowed to do everything men could do—including wearing pants. The baggy pants she wore were called "bloomers" in her honor, and that's what they've been called ever since.

STATE SONG

Many songs have been written about New York. The state song, "I Love New York," was written in 1977 as part of a campaign to promote tourism in the state. Another well-known song, "New York, Our Empire State," celebrates the state's wealth of natural resources. It was dedicated to the New York Federation of Music Club.

NEW YORK, OUR EMPIRE STATE

Music by Etta H. Morris; lyrics by Caroline Fitzsimmons

Oh New York State, All hail to thee! Dear land of hope and liberty! Thy fertile fields, thy green clad hills, And fruited orchards' beauty thrills. Thy rivers shining in the sun, From pearly lakes to ocean run, Thy harbors deep and calm and wide And haven for the ships outside. Oh Empire State.

A NEW YORK RECIPE

New York cheesecake is unique because of its extra ingredient—sour cream. This recipe is a classic from old-fashioned New York delis.

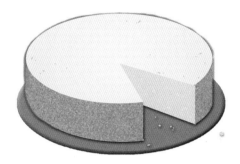

NEW YORK CHEESECAKE

One 9-inch springform pan
1 prepared cheesecake crust
15 crushed graham crackers
2 tablespoons of melted butter
32 ounces of cream cheese
1½ cups of white sugar

¾ cup of milk
4 eggs
1 cup of sour cream
1 tablespoon of vanilla extract
¼ cup of flour

1. Have an adult preheat the oven to 350° F.
2. Grease the springform pan.
3. Mix the graham cracker crumbs with the melted butter in a small bowl.
4. Press graham cracker/butter mixture onto the bottom of springform pan.
5. In a large bowl, mix cream cheese with sugar until mixture is smooth.
6. Pour in milk and stir slowly.
7. Add eggs one at a time, stirring just enough to combine.
8. Mix in flour, vanilla, and sour cream until smooth.
9. Pour entire mixture into prepared cheesecake crust.
10. Bake for one hour in the preheated oven.
11. After one hour, turn the oven off and let the cake cool inside the oven with the door closed for 5 to 6 hours.

HISTORICAL TIMELINE

8,000 B.C.   The first people arrive in what later became New York.

A.D. 1400s   The Iroquois Confederacy is formed.

1524   Giovanni da Verrazano sails into what later became New York City.

1609   Henry Hudson explores the Hudson River and claims the region for the Dutch. It is called New Netherland.

1624   Dutch settlers establish a colony at Fort Orange (later Albany).

1664   Britain takes over New Netherland and renames it New York.

1689   The French and Indian Wars begin between France and England. Many battles occur in the New York area.

1763   The French and Indian Wars end.

1765   American colonists boycott British goods to protest new taxes.

1775   The American War of Independence (1775–1781) begins.

1777 The colonists win their first major victory, the Battle of Saratoga, in New York.

1788 New York becomes the 11th state to join the Union.

1812 New York is the site of several battles in the War of 1812 (1812–1814).

1825 The Erie Canal, which connects Lake Erie to the Hudson River, is completed.

1861 The Civil War (1861–1865) begins. New York joins the Northern side.

1900 Immigrants pour into New York. One out of every three New Yorkers has been born in a foreign country.

1929 The stock market crashes, and the Great Depression begins.

1932 Franklin Roosevelt is elected president. He establishes an economic program to help lead the country out of the Great Depression.

1990 A museum is opened at the former immigration station on Ellis Island.

2001 On September 11, two hijacked planes crash into New York City's World Trade Center, causing the collapse of its twin towers. Thousands of people died in the worst terrorist attack in history.

OUTSTANDING NEW YORKERS

Susan B. Anthony

Lucille Ball

Irving Berlin

Kareem Abdul-Jabbar (born 1947), originally named Lewis Alcindor, is recognized as one of the best basketball players ever. During his 20-year career, he played for the Milwaukee Bucks and the Los Angeles Lakers. At 7 feet 2 inches, he was a giant on the basketball court, leading his teams to six NBA championship titles.

Susan B. Anthony (1820–1906) was a pioneer crusader for women's rights in the United States. Her work helped pave the way for the Nineteenth Amendment, which gave women the right to vote. She lived her adult life in Rochester, New York.

Lucille Ball (1911–1989) was a famous comedienne and entertainer. She played the funny homemaker Lucy Ricardo in the popular 1950s television show *I Love Lucy.* She was born in Jamestown, New York, and began her career in New York City.

Irving Berlin (1888–1989), a self-taught musician, composed many popular songs. His most famous are "God Bless America" and "White Christmas." Berlin moved to New York City when he was a young boy.

Leonard Bernstein (1918–1990) was a famous American composer and conductor. He composed many musicals, including *West Side Story.* He was also the first American to become the musical director of the New York Philharmonic Orchestra.

Tom Cruise (born 1962), a popular movie actor, is from Syracuse, New York. He has starred in many major films, including *Top Gun, Jerry Maguire, Mission: Impossible,* and *Magnolia.*

Tom Cruise

Deganawida (1550?–1600?), a Huron Indian, teamed up with Iroquois leader Hiawatha to develop the Law of Peace, an agreement that led to peace among the Iroquois tribes. Deganawida, also known as the Peacemaker, lived most of his life in what later became western New York.

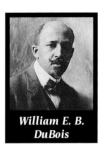

William E. B. DuBois (1868–1963) was a writer, educator, and civil rights leader. Born in Great Barrington, he attended Harvard University and later edited *Crisis*, the magazine of the National Association for the Advancement of Colored People (NAACP).

Ezra Jack Keats

Ezra Jack Keats (1916–1983) was an author and illustrator of children's books. Keats came from New York City and is known for his illustrations containing collages. He won the Caldecott Medal for *The Snowy Day* in 1963.

Spike Lee (born 1957) grew up in Brooklyn, New York. He has directed many movies, including *Do the Right Thing*, *Get on the Bus*, and *Summer of Sam*. He is known for his fast-paced, colorful movies that explore race relations.

Spike Lee

Madeleine L'Engle (born 1918) is best known for her books for children and young adults. In 1963 she won the Newbery Medal for her children's book *A Wrinkle in Time*. Other popular books include *Meet the Austins*, *A Ring of Endless Light*, and *A House Like a Lotus*. L'Engle was born in New York City.

Madeleine L'Engle

Grandma Moses

Grandma Moses (1860–1961), whose real name was Anna Mary Robertson, didn't take up painting until she was 76 years old. Although she never took an art lesson, she gained fame painting simple pictures of country life. She was born in Greenwich.

Rosie O'Donnell

Rosie O'Donnell (born 1962) is a comedienne who created her own daytime television talk show, *The Rosie O'Donnell Show*, in New York City. She has also starred in a Broadway play and several movies, including *A League of Their Own*, *The Flintstones*, and *Harriet the Spy*. O'Donnell was raised on Long Island.

J. Robert Oppenheimer (1904–1967), known as the Father of the Atom Bomb, was born in New York City. He was director of the laboratory in Los Alamos, New Mexico, where the first atomic bomb was made in the 1940s. He later supported arms control and opposed the development of the hydrogen bomb, a very powerful type of atomic bomb, because of the huge risks it posed.

John D. Rockefeller

John D. Rockefeller (1839–1937), from Richford, New York, was a businessman who made his fortune in the oil business. He helped form the Standard Oil Company in 1870. Rockefeller gave away more than $500 million to help other people and organizations.

Norman Rockwell (1894–1978) is one of the best-loved artists in the United States. Many of his paintings show humorous scenes from everyday life. Rockwell was born in New York City.

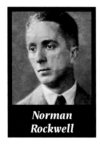

Norman Rockwell

Eleanor Roosevelt (1884–1962) was the niece of President Theodore Roosevelt and the wife of President Franklin Delano Roosevelt, but she distinguished herself on her own as a social reformer. As first lady during the Great Depression and World War II, she played an active role in politics. Through her work as a speaker, writer, and diplomat, she fought for social justice in the United States and around the world. She was born in New York City.

Theodore Roosevelt (1858–1919), from New York City, was vice president of the United States at the time of President William McKinley's assassination in 1901. He became the youngest president in U.S. history. Roosevelt loved the outdoors and established the United States Forest Service, along with numerous national forests and national monuments.

Roger Straus Jr.

Roger Straus Jr. (born 1917) founded the highly successful publishing company Farrar, Straus and Giroux in 1946, after serving in the U.S. Navy during World War II. Farrar, Straus and Giroux has published 20 Nobel laureates, 12 Pulitzer Prize–winners, and many winners of Caldecott and Newbery medals for children's literature. Straus was born in New York City.

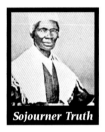

Sojourner Truth

Sojourner Truth (1797?–1883) was named Isabelle when she was born into slavery in Ulster County, New York. After slavery was abolished in New York State in 1827, she took the name Sojourner Truth and became known as a great speechmaker. She spoke out against slavery and for women's rights.

Edith Wharton

Edith Wharton (1862–1937) was the author of more than 50 books, including short stories, travel books, and historical novels. Best known for her stories about New England upper-class society, her most famous works are *The Age of Innocence*, which won a Pulitzer Prize, and *Ethan Frome*. Wharton was born in New York City.

Walt Whitman (1819–1892) was born in West Hills on Long Island, New York, and grew up in Brooklyn. A poet, Whitman's most famous book is *Leaves of Grass*. He praised the United States and democracy in his poems.

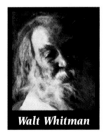

Walt Whitman

FACTS-AT-A-GLANCE

Nickname: The Empire State

Song: "I Love New York"

Motto: *Excelsior* (Ever Upward)

Flower: rose

Tree: sugar maple

Bird: bluebird

Animal: beaver

Fruit: apple

Gem: garnet

Insect: ladybug

Date and ranking of statehood: July 26, 1788, the 11th state

Capital: Albany

Area: 47,224 square miles

Rank in area, nationwide: 30th

Average January temperature: 21° F

Average July temperature: 69° F

New York's flag was adopted in 1909. It features two women, Liberty and Justice, who are holding a shield. The state motto also graces the flag.

POPULATION GROWTH

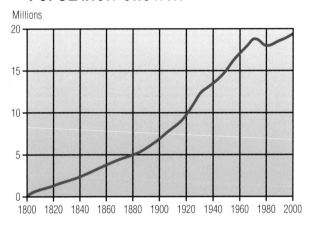

Millions

This chart shows how New York's population has grown from 1800 to 2000.

In use since 1882, the New York state seal shows the state shield. A mountain landscape, golden sunlight, and a ship on a river appear on the shield. The seal is also on the state flag.

Population: 18,976,457 (2000 Census)

Rank in population, nationwide: 3rd

Major cities and populations: (2000 Census) New York (8,008,278), Buffalo (292,648), Rochester (219,773), Yonkers (196,086), Syracuse (147,306), Albany (95,658)

U.S. senators: 2

U.S. representatives: 29

Electoral votes: 31

Natural resources: emery, fertile soil, forests, granite, limestone, natural gas, petroleum, salt, sand and gravel, sandstone, water

Agricultural products: apples, beef and dairy cattle, cabbages, eggs, grapes, hogs, maple syrup, milk, potatoes, poultry, sheep, snap beans, sweet corn

Fishing: clams, eels, flounder, lobster, oyster, scallops, sea trout, striped bass, walleye, whiting, yellow perch

Manufactured goods: cameras, chemicals, clothing, dental equipment, electrical equipment, machinery, photographic film, printed materials

WHERE NEW YORKERS WORK

Services—71 percent (services includes jobs in trade; community, social, and personal services: finance, insurance, and real estate; transportation, communication, and utilities)

Government—14 percent

Manufacturing—10 percent

Construction—4 percent

Agriculture—1 percent

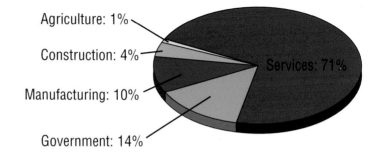

Agriculture: 1%
Construction: 4%
Manufacturing: 10%
Government: 14%
Services: 71%

GROSS STATE PRODUCT

Services—74 percent

Government—11 percent

Manufacturing—11 percent

Construction—3 percent

Agriculture—1 percent

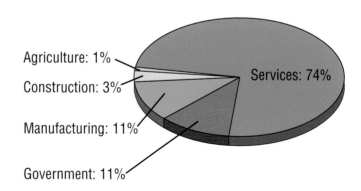

Agriculture: 1%
Construction: 3%
Manufacturing: 11%
Government: 11%
Services: 74%

NEW YORK WILDLIFE

Mammals: beaver, chipmunk, coyote, eastern black bear, muskrat, opossum, porcupine, rabbit, rat, red fox, skunk, squirrel, whales, white-tailed deer, wildcats, woodchuck

Birds: bald eagle, bluebird, Canada goose, common loon, egret, golden eagle, grouse, hawks, owls, partridge, peregrine falcon, pheasant, quail, tern, wild turkey, wood duck

Amphibians and reptiles: Massasauga, mudpuppy, mud turtle, rattlesnake, spotted salamander, toads, turtles

Fish: bass, bluefish, bluegill, clams, crabs, flounder, oyster, perch, pike, salmon, shad, sharks, sunfish, swordfish

Trees: balsam fir, beech, black cherry, oak, pine, spruce, sugar maple, yellow birch

Wild plants: black-eyed Susan, bleedingheart, buttercup, curly grass, devil's paintbrush, enchanter's nightshade, goldenrod, goldenthread, Indian pipe, Queen Anne's lace, starflower, trillium, violet, water lilies, wild roses

The bluebird is New York's state bird.

PLACES TO VISIT

American Museum of Natural History, New York City
This museum houses exhibits about dinosaurs, whales, birds, snakes, and sea life. It also includes the newly-built Rose Center for Earth and Space and the Gottesman Hall of Planet Earth.

Central Park, New York City
This 843-acre oasis of green space in the heart of Manhattan is home to a children's zoo, athletic fields, playgrounds, gardens, woods, ponds, and more. Designed by famous landscape architect Frederick Law Olmsted, Central Park has been open since 1859.

Empire State Building, New York City
Completed in 1931, the Empire State Building was the tallest building in the world for many years. Rising 102 stories above ground, its observation decks offer visitors a spectacular view of the city.

Fort Ticonderoga, Lake Champlain
This reconstructed colonial fort marks the site of an important victory for the Americans during the Revolutionary War. It was here that colonist Ethan Allen and his Green Mountain Boys defeated British troops in 1775.

Metropolitan Museum of Art, New York City
The largest art museum in the United States, the Met occupies four city blocks and houses more than 2 million works of art.

National Baseball Hall of Fame, Cooperstown

If you're a baseball fan, this is the place to visit. The Hall of Fame honors the game's great players and includes exhibits on the history of baseball.

New York State Museum, Albany

The oldest state museum in the nation, this museum's collections include natural history, science, and the art and history of New York.

Niagara Falls

This favorite tourist spot consists of two waterfalls on the border between Canada and the United States—the American Falls and the Horseshoe Falls. Parks line both sides of the river, and tourists can take a boat ride to the base of the falls.

Statue of Liberty National Monument, New York Harbor

The Upper New York Bay is home to this famous national statue. The monument also includes Ellis Island, which was the inspection station and temporary shelter for millions of immigrants hoping to enter the United States.

Watkins Glen State Park, Watkins Glen

The most famous of the Finger Lakes State Parks, this park boasts 18 water-falls along the glen's stream.

Quiet spots, such as Central Park in New York City, can be found in many of New York's urban areas.

ANNUAL EVENTS

Ice Castle Extravaganza, Mayville—*February*

Westminster Kennel Club Dog Show, New York City—*February*

Syracuse Winterfest—*February*

Saint Patrick's Day Parade, New York City—*March*

Festival of Gold, Niagara County—*April–May*

Great New York State Fair, Syracuse—*August–September*

Adirondack Hot Air Balloon Festival, Glens Falls—*September*

Macy's Thanksgiving Day Parade, New York City—*November*

A Festival of Lights, Niagara Falls—*November–January*

LEARN MORE ABOUT NEW YORK

BOOKS

General

Avakian, Monique. *A Historical Album of New York.* Brookfield, CT:
Millbrook Press, 1993.

Fradin, Dennis Brindell. *New York.* Chicago: Children's Press, 1993.

Heinrichs, Ann. *New York.* Chicago: Children's Press, 1999.
For older readers.

Special Interest

Doherty, Craig and Katherine M. Doherty. *The Empire State Building.*
Woodbridge, CT: Blackbirch Press, 1998. The history of the
Empire State Building is retold through text and photos.
Special emphasis is given to architecture, engineering, and
construction of the building.

Mann, Elizabeth. *The Brooklyn Bridge.* New York: Mikaya Press,
1996. Learn more about the construction of the Brooklyn
Bridge—from its conception by John Roebling, through its many
setbacks, to its completion under the direction of Roebling's son
in 1883.

Shenandoah-Tekalihwa, Joanne, and Douglas M. George-
Kanentiio. *Skywoman: Legends of the Iroquois.* Santa Fe, NM:
Clear Light Publishers, 1998. Two Native American writers

tell the ancient stories of the Iroquois peoples, including the Iroquois creation story and the story of the Iroquois Peacemaker.

Fiction

Bruchac, Joseph. *The Arrow Over the Door.* New York: Dial Books, 1998. In 1777 a 14-year-old Quaker boy from Saratoga, New York, meets a young Abenaki Indian who is on a scouting mission for the British army. Based on a real incident, the story is a reminder that fear and prejudice can be overcome.

Konigsburg, E. L. *From the Mixed-Up Files of Mrs. Basil E. Frankweiler.* New York: Atheneum, 1970. Claudia and her brother run away to the Metropolitan Museum of Art, where they encounter mystery and adventure. Konigsburg won the Newbery Medal for this delightful book in 1967.

Quackenbush, Robert M. *Daughter of Liberty: A True Story of the American Revolution.* New York: Hyperion, 1999. The colonists are fighting Great Britain in the War of Independence when Wyn accepts a dangerous mission from General George Washington that will help defeat the British.

Selden, George. *The Cricket in Times Square.* New York: Farrar Straus & Giroux, 1983. Chester, a cricket from quiet Connecticut, finds himself living in a subway station in busy New York City. He experiences urban life along with his friends Tucker Mouse, Harry Cat, and Mario. First published in 1960, this Newbery Honor book features illustrations by Garth Williams.

Smith, Betty. *A Tree Grows in Brooklyn.* New York: Perennial Classics, 1998. Older readers learn about life in Brooklyn, New York, during the early 1900s. Francie and her family struggle with poverty, hunger, sick neighbors, and alcoholism. First published in 1943.

Stevens, Carla. *Anna, Grandpa, and the Big Storm.* New York: Penguin Putnam, 1998. During the blizzard of 1888, the whole city of New York is covered in snow. Anna and her grandfather are trying to get to school for the final day of the spelling bee. The two become stranded on the Third Avenue elevated train.

WEBSITES

New York State Homepage
<http://www.state.ny.us>
New York's official website includes information about the Empire State's government agencies, education and social programs, and environmental issues.

I Love New York
<http://www.iloveny.state.ny.us>
Learn about New York's many attractions, upcoming events, vacation possibilities, and much more.

The New York Times on the Web
<http://www.nytimes.com>
With a daily circulation of more than 1 million readers, the *New York Times* is one of the largest newspapers in the United States. Explore the site for New York's news, as well as national and international events.

PRONUNCIATION GUIDE

Adirondack (ad-uh-RAHN-dak)

Algonquian (al-GAHN-kwee-uhn)

Appalachian (ap-uh-LAY-chuhn)

Iroquois (IHR-uh-kwoy)

Mahican (muh-HEE-kuhn)

Montauk (MAHN-tawk)

Oneida (oh-NYD-uh)

Seneca (SEHN-ih-kuh)

Stuyvesant, Peter (STY-vuh-suhnt, PEET-ur)

Syracuse (SIHR-uh-kyoos)

Tuscarora (tuhs-kuh-ROHR-uh)

Wappinger (WAH-pihn-jur)

Since 1883 opera singers have entertained music lovers at the Metropolitan Opera House in New York City.

GLOSSARY

borough: one of the five counties of New York City. The five boroughs are the Bronx, Brooklyn, Manhattan, Queens, and Staten Island.

boycott: to refuse to buy, sell, or use something

colony: a territory ruled by a country some distance away

Great Lakes: a chain of five lakes in Canada and the northern United States. They are Lakes Erie, Huron, Michigan, Ontario, and Superior.

groundwater: water that lies beneath the earth's surface. The water comes from rain and snow that seep through soil into the cracks and other openings in rocks. Groundwater supplies wells and springs.

immigrant: a person who moves into a foreign country and settles there

landfill: a place specially prepared for burying solid waste

leachate: liquid formed by the decomposition of waste in a landfill

Loyalist: a person who supports the government during a revolt

melting pot: a place where people of many different nationalities and races live and blend

reservation: public land set aside by the government to be used by Native Americans

rural: having to do with the countryside or farming

stock: a share in the ownership of a business. Stocks are bought and sold at stock exchanges.

INDEX

PHOTO ACKNOWLEDGMENTS

Cover photographs by © Charles E. Rotkin/CORBIS (left) and © Joseph Sohm; ChromoSohm Inc./CORBIS (right); PresentationMaps.com, pp. 1, 8, 9, 50; © L. Clarke/CORBIS, pp. 2–3; © David Muench/CORBIS, pp. 3, 6; Bruce Burkhardt/CORBIS, pp. 4, 7, 18, 42, 54; © Richard T. Nowitz/CORBIS, p. 7; © Gerry Lemmo, pp. 10, 13, 29, 73; New York State Department of Economic Development, pp. 11, 41, 49, 52; © Hubert Stadler/CORBIS, p. 12; Hudson River Valley Association, pp. 14, 22; © Mark L. Stephenson/CORBIS, p. 15; Betty Groskin, pp. 16, 57; Monica V. Brown, Photographic Artist, pp. 17, 45; New-York Historical Society, New York City, pp. 19, 21, 23, 30, 32; Picture Collection, The Branch Libraries, The New York Public Library, p. 20; Library of Congress, pp. 24, 33, 35, 38, 61, 66 (top), 67 (top), 68 (bottom); Fenimore Art Museum, Cooperstown, New York, p. 25; The Brooklyn Historical Society, p. 28; © Kit Kittle/CORBIS, p. 34; Tony LaGruth, pp. 36, 75; © Schenectady Museum, Hall of Electrical History Foundation/CORBIS, p. 37; © Underwood & Underwood/CORBIS, p. 39; © Jeff Greenberg/Photo Agora, p. 43; © Bettmann/CORBIS, pp. 44, 69 (middle bottom); © Dave G. Houser/CORBIS, p. 46; © Duomo/CORBIS, p. 47; Eliot J. Schechter/Allsport, p. 48; James Blank/Root Resources, pp. 51, 53; James Mejuto Photo, pp. 55, 58; © Arthur Morris/Visuals Unlimited, p. 56; NYC Department of Sanitation, p. 59; Jack Lindstrom, p. 60; Tim Seeley, pp. 63, 71, 72; Independent Picture Service, pp. 66 (middle top), 68 (middle bottom); Hollywood Book and Poster, Inc., pp. 66 (middle bottom, bottom), 67 (middle bottom); © James Phillips, p. 67 (bottom); National Archives, p. 68 (top); © Mitchell Gerber/CORBIS, p. 68 (middle top); © Gasper Tringale, p. 69 (top); Minneapolis Public Library and Information Center, p. 69 (middle top); The Pennsylvania Academy of the Fine Arts, p. 69 (bottom); Jean Matheny, p. 70 (top); Metropolitan Opera/Winnie Klotz, p. 80.